The Testament of Abraham

By Abraham

Copyright © 2020 Lamp of Trismegistus. All rights reserved. No part of this publication may be reproduced or transmitted in any form or by any means, electronic or mechanical, including photocopying, recording, or by any information storage and retrieval system, without permission in writing from Lamp of Trismegistus. Reviewers may quote brief passages.

ISBN: 978-1-63118-441-3

Christian Apocrypha Series

Other Books in this Series and Related Titles

Book of Dreams by Enoch (978-1-63118-437-6)

The Book of Astronomical Secrets by Enoch (978-1-63118-443-7)

Psalms of Solomon by King Solomon (978-1-63118-439-0)

The Lives of Adam and Eve by Moses (978-1-63118-414-7)

The First and Second Gospels of the Infancy of Jesus Christ by Thomas and James (978-1-63118-415-4)

Lost Chapters of the Book of Daniel and Related Writings by Daniel (978-1-63118-417-8)

The Testament of Moses by Moses (978-1-63118-440-6)

The Book of the Watchers by Enoch (978-1-63118-416-1)

The Book of Parables by Enoch (978-1-63118-429-1)

Masonic Symbolism of Easter and the Christ in Masonry by various authors (978-1-63118-434-5)

A Few Masonic Sermons by A. C. Ward & Bascom B. Clarke (978-1-63118-435-2)

Masonic Symbolism of King Solomon's Temple by Albert G. Mackey & others (978-1-63118-442-0)

Cloud Upon the Sanctuary by A. E. Waite & K. Eckartshausen (978-1-63118-438-3)

The Two Great Pillars of Boaz and Jachin by Albert G. Mackey & others (978-1-63118-433-8)

Audio Versions are also Available on Audible and iTunes

Table of Contents

Introduction...7

Prologue...9

Chapter I...11

Chapter II...13

Chapter III...15

Chapter IV...17

Chapter V...19

Chapter VI...21

Chapter VII...23

Chapter VIII...25

Chapter XIX...27

Chapter X...29

Chapter XI...31

Chapter XII...33

Chapter XIII...35

Chapter XIV...37

Chapter XV…39

Chapter XVI…41

Chapter XVII…43

Chapter XVIII…45

Chapter XIX…47

Chapter XX…49

Introduction

The Apocrypha are a loosely knit series of books, written by early vanguards of Christianity (covering the eras of both the old and new testaments), and which comprise somewhere between about a dozen to several hundred titles, depending on whom you ask and how that person defines "Apocrypha." A small selection of these can still be found included in the Catholic bible, while a majority of the books in question, were abandoned by church officials in the early centuries of Christianity. Many of these apocryphal books were originally considered canon by early followers of Christ, in the first four centuries following his birth. It wasn't until the meeting of the Council of Nicaea in 325, that Emperor Constantine and a group of roughly 300 church bishops, gathered together with the goal of defining, standardizing and unifying an otherwise splintering Christianity, that many of these writings ceased to be included in the newly established canon. Enjoy then, this book as an example, of just one of the many books of the Christian Apocrypha, and be sure to check out other titles in this series.

Prologue

The Testament of Abraham was likely written originally in Greek, by someone living in Egypt at the time. This is due to the fact that the vocabulary found in the text is quite similar to the vocabulary used in the later books of the Septuagint, which were being written at that time, in addition to other books, such as 3 Maccabees, that we know were written around that time in Egypt. In addition, there are aspects of the story that seem to reflect aspects of Egyptian life, such as the three judgments which mirror the three levels of Egyptian government.

In an overall sense, this testament deals with Abraham's reluctance to die and the means by which his death was brought about.

As for the specific content, the story interestingly deals with Death in the form of the embodiment in an angel, much like the classically depicted Grim Reaper.

It begins with God telling the angel Michael to "Go down ... to my friend Abraham and speak to him concerning death, so that he might put his affairs in order." Michael comes down to earth and finds Abraham, and the two greet each other; however, Abraham believes Michael to be an ordinary man. Michael returns to Heaven and tells God that Abraham is too nice—Michael is unable to tell Abraham of his death. God promises instead, to send a dream to Isaac that will show Abraham's death. Michael comes back down to Earth and eats dinner with Abraham. Isaac then goes to sleep and dreams of Abraham's death, though the contents of the dream are not discussed yet. Sarah recognizes Michael as one of the angels in Genesis 18, and Abraham confirms this by remembering Michael. Isaac explains his dream, and Michael then orders Abraham to put his affairs in order; however, Abraham refuses and wants to be shown the world before he dies. God agrees and Abraham is shown the world and heaven. While in heaven he is shown where souls are judged, and interestingly, he is shown one soul that is perfectly balanced between good and evil. Abraham prays for this balanced soul. After Abraham refuses to go with Michael a second time, God sends Death. Death arrives in disguise but eventually reveals himself and takes the life of Abraham.

When viewed as a religious text, the Testament of Abraham gives a unique message. Beyond the presence of angels and God and Death, the lessons which are highlighted are simply about being a good person, performing good acts, as well as avoiding bad ones. In the scenes of judgment, there is no distinction made between whether people are Jewish or Gentile, only whether they have performed good deeds or bad. This leaves the reader with the understanding that he should behave toward others with universally fair treatment, not treatment which is influenced by lineage or any other ethnic traits. As well, when it comes to judgment where a person whose sins outweigh their good deeds, they will be sentenced to eternal punishment, while one whose good deeds outweigh their sins will move on to paradise, and this will be the case independent of their race or beliefs.

Chapter I

Abraham lived the measure of his life, nine hundred and ninety-five years, and having lived all the years of his life in quietness, gentleness, and righteousness, the righteous one was exceeding hospitable; for, pitching his tent in the cross-ways at the oak of Mamre, he received every one, both rich and poor, kings and rulers, the maimed and the helpless, friends and strangers, neighbors and travelers, all alike did the devout, all-holy, righteous, and hospitable Abraham entertain. Even upon him, however, there came the common, inexorable, bitter lot of death, and the uncertain end of life. Therefore the Lord God, summoning his archangel Michael, said to him: Go down, chief-captain Michael, to Abraham and speak to him concerning his death, that he may set his affairs in order, for I have blessed him as the stars of heaven, and as the sand by the sea-shore, and he is in abundance of long life and many possessions, and is becoming exceeding rich. Beyond all men, moreover, he is righteous in every goodness, hospitable and loving to the end of his life; but go, archangel Michael, to Abraham, my beloved friend, and announce to him his death and assure him thus: You shall at this time depart from this vain world, and shall quit the body, and go to your own Lord among the good.

Chapter II

And the chief-captain departed from before the face of God, and went down to Abraham to the oak of Mamre, and found the righteous Abraham in the field close by, sitting beside yokes of oxen for ploughing, together with the sons of Masek and other servants, to the number of twelve. And behold the chief-captain came to him, and Abraham, seeing the chief-captain Michael coming from afar, like to a very comely warrior, arose and met him as was his custom, meeting and entertaining all strangers. And the chief-captain saluted him and said: Hail, most honored father, righteous soul chosen of God, true son of the heavenly one. Abraham said to the chief-captain: Hail, most honored warrior, bright as the sun and most beautiful above all the sons of men; you are welcome; therefore I beseech your presence, tell me whence the youth of your age has come; teach me, your suppliant, whence and from what army and from what journey your beauty has come hither. The chief-captain said: I, O righteous Abraham, come from the great city. I have been sent by the great king to take the place of a good friend of his, for the king has summoned him. And Abraham said, Come, my Lord, go with me as far as my field. The chief-captain said: I come; and going into the field of the ploughing, they sat down beside the company. And Abraham said to his servants, the sons of Masek: Go to the herd of horses, and bring two horses, quiet, and gentle and tame, so that I and this stranger may sit thereon. But the chief-captain said, Nay, my Lord, Abraham, let them not bring horses, for I abstain from ever sitting upon any four-footed beast. Is not my king rich in much merchandise, having power both over men and all kinds of cattle? But I abstain from ever sitting upon any four-footed beast. Let us go, then, O righteous soul, walking lightly until we reach your house. And Abraham said, Amen, be it so.

Chapter III

And as they went on from the field toward his house, beside that way there stood a cypress tree, and by the command of the Lord the tree cried out with a human voice, saying, Holy, holy, holy is the Lord God that calls himself to those that love him; but Abraham hid the mystery, thinking that the chief-captain had not heard the voice of the tree. And coming near to the house they sat down in the court, and Isaac seeing the face of the angel said to Sarah his mother, My lady mother, behold, the man sitting with my father Abraham is not a son of the race of those that dwell on the earth. And Isaac ran, and saluted him, and fell at the feet of the Incorporeal, and the Incorporeal blessed him and said, The Lord God will grant you his promise that he made to your father Abraham and to his seed, and will also grant you the precious prayer of your father and your mother. Abraham said to Isaac his son, My son Isaac, draw water from the well, and bring it me in the vessel, that we may wash the feet of this stranger, for he is tired, having come to us from off a long journey. And Isaac ran to the well and drew water in the vessel and brought it to them, and Abraham went up and washed the feet of the chief captain Michael, and the heart of Abraham was moved, and he wept over the stranger. And Isaac, seeing his father weeping, wept also, and the chief captain, seeing them weeping, also wept with them, and the tears of the chief captain fell upon the vessel into the water of the basin and became precious stones. And Abraham seeing the marvel, and being astonished, took the stones secretly, and hid the mystery, keeping it by himself in his heart.

Chapter IV

And Abraham said to Isaac his son: Go, my beloved son, into the inner chamber of the house and beautify it. Spread for us there two couches, one for me and one for this man that is guest with us this day. Prepare for us there a seat and a candlestick and a table with abundance of every good thing. Beautify the chamber, my son, and spread under us linen and purple and fine linen. Burn there every precious and excellent incense, and bring sweet-smelling plants from the garden and fill our house with them. Kindle seven lamps full of oil, so that we may rejoice, for this man that is our guest this day is more glorious than kings or rulers, and his appearance surpasses all the sons of men. And Isaac prepared all things well, and Abraham taking the archangel Michael went into the chamber, and they both sat down upon the couches, and between them he placed a table with abundance of every good thing. Then the chief captain arose and went out, as if by constraint of his belly to make issue of water, and ascended to heaven in the twinkling of an eye, and stood before the Lord, and said to him: Lord and Master, let your power know that I am unable to remind that righteous man of his death, for I have not seen upon the earth a man like him, pitiful, hospitable, righteous, truthful, devout, refraining from every evil deed. And now know, Lord, that I cannot remind him of his death. And the Lord said: Go down, chief-captain Michael, to my friend Abraham, and do whatever he says to you, and eat with him whatever he eats. And I will send my Holy Spirit upon his son Isaac, and will put the remembrance of his death into the heart of Isaac, so that even he in a dream may see the death of his father, and Isaac will relate the dream, and you shall interpret it, and he himself will know his end. And the chief-captain said, Lord, all the heavenly spirits are incorporeal, and neither eat nor drink, and this man has set before me a table with abundance of all good things earthly and corruptible. Now, Lord, what shall I do? How shall I escape him, sitting at one table with him? The Lord said: Go down to him, and take no thought for this, for when you sit down with him, I will send upon you a devouring spirit, and it will consume out of your hands and through your mouth all that is on the table. Rejoice together with him in everything, only you shall interpret well the things of the vision, that Abraham may know the sickle of death and the uncertain end of life, and may make disposal of all his possessions, for I have blessed him above the sand of the sea and as the stars of heaven.

Chapter V

Then the chief captain went down to the house of Abraham, and sat down with him at the table, and Isaac served them. And when the supper was ended, Abraham prayed after his custom, and the chief-captain prayed together with him, and each lay down to sleep upon his couch. And Isaac said to his father, Father, I too would fain sleep with you in this chamber, that I also may hear your discourse, for I love to hear the excellence of the conversation of this virtuous man. Abraham said, Nay, my son, but go to your own chamber and sleep on your own couch, lest we be troublesome to this man. Then Isaac, having received the prayer from them, and having blessed them, went to his own chamber and lay down upon his couch. But the Lord cast the thought of death into the heart of Isaac as in a dream, and about the third hour of the night Isaac awoke and rose up from his couch, and came running to the chamber where his father was sleeping together with the archangel. Isaac, therefore, on reaching the door cried out, saying, My father Abraham, arise and open to me quickly, that I may enter and hang upon your neck, and embrace you before they take you away from me. Abraham therefore arose and opened to him, and Isaac entered and hung upon his neck, and began to weep with a loud voice. Abraham therefore being moved at heart, also wept with a loud voice, and the chief-captain, seeing them weeping, wept also. Sarah being in her room, heard their weeping, and came running to them, and found them embracing and weeping. And Sarah said with weeping, My Lord Abraham, what is this that you weep? Tell me, my Lord, has this brother that has been entertained by us this day brought you tidings of Lot, your brother's son, that he is dead? Is it for this that you grieve thus? The chief-captain answered and said to her, Nay, my sister Sarah, it is not as you say, but your son Isaac, methinks, beheld a dream, and came to us weeping, and we seeing him were moved in our hearts and wept.

Chapter VI

Then Sarah, hearing the excellence of the conversation of the chief-captain, straightway knew that it was an angel of the Lord that spoke. Sarah therefore signified to Abraham to come out towards the door, and said to him, My Lord Abraham, do you know who this man is? Abraham said, I know not. Sarah said, You know, my Lord, the three men from heaven that were entertained by us in our tent beside the oak of Mamre, when you killed the kid without blemish, and set a table before them. After the flesh had been eaten, the kid rose again, and sucked its mother with great joy. Do you not know, my Lord Abraham, that by promise they gave to us Isaac as the fruit of the womb? Of these three holy men this is one. Abraham said, O Sarah, in this you speak the truth. Glory and praise from our God and the Father. For late in the evening when I washed his feet in the basin I said in my heart, These are the feet of one of the three men that I washed then; and his tears that fell into the basin then became precious stones. And shaking them out from his lap he gave them to Sarah, saying, If you believe me not, look now at these. And Sarah receiving them bowed down and saluted and said, Glory be to God that shows us wonderful things. And now know, my Lord Abraham, that there is among us the revelation of something, whether it be evil or good!

Chapter VII

And Abraham left Sarah, and went into the chamber, and said to Isaac, Come hither, my beloved son, tell me the truth, what it was you saw and what befell you that you came so hastily to us. And Isaac answering began to say, I saw, my Lord, in this night the sun and the moon above my head, surrounding me with its rays and giving me light. As I gazed at this and rejoiced, I saw the heaven opened, and a man bearing light descend from it, shining more than seven suns. And this man like the sun came and took away the sun from my head, and went up into the heavens from whence he came, but I was greatly grieved that he took away the sun from me. After a little, as I was still sorrowing and sore troubled, I saw this man come forth from heaven a second time, and he took away from me the moon also from off my head, and I wept greatly and called upon that man of light, and said, Do not, my Lord, take away my glory from me; pity me and hear me, and if you take away the sun from me, then leave the moon to me. He said, Suffer them to be taken up to the king above, for he wishes them there. And he took them away from me, but he left the rays upon me. The chief-captain said, Hear, O righteous Abraham; the sun which your son saw is you his father, and the moon likewise is Sarah his mother. The man bearing light who descended from heaven, this is the one sent from God who is to take your righteous soul from you. And now know, O most honored Abraham, that at this time you shall leave this worldly life, and remove to God. Abraham said to the chief captain O strangest of marvels! And now are you he that shall take my soul from me? The chief-captain said to him, I am the chief-captain Michael, that stands before the Lord, and I was sent to you to remind you of your death, and then I shall depart to him as I was commanded. Abraham said, Now I know that you are an angel of the Lord, and wast sent to take my soul, but I will not go with you; but do whatever you are commanded.

Chapter VIII

The chief-captain hearing these words immediately vanished, and ascending into heaven stood before God, and told all that he had seen in the house of Abraham; and the chief-captain said this also to his Lord, Thus says your friend Abraham, I will not go with you, but do whatever you are commanded; and now, O Lord Almighty, does your glory and immortal kingdom order anything? God said to the chief-captain Michael, Go to my friend Abraham yet once again, and speak to him thus, Thus says the Lord your God, he that brought you into the land of promise, that blessed you above the sand of the sea and above the stars of heaven, that opened the womb of barrenness of Sarah, and granted you Isaac as the fruit of the womb in old age, Verily I say unto you that blessing I will bless you, and multiplying I will multiply your seed, and I will give you all that you shall ask from me, for I am the Lord your God, and besides me there is no other. Tell me why you have rebelled against me, and why there is grief in you, and why you rebelled against my archangel Michael? Do you not know that all who have come from Adam and Eve have died, and that none of the prophets has escaped death? None of those that rule as kings is immortal; none of your forefathers has escaped the mystery of death. They have all died, they have all departed into Hades, they are all gathered by the sickle of death. But upon you I have not sent death, I have not suffered any deadly disease to come upon you, I have not permitted the sickle of death to meet you, I have not allowed the nets of

Hades to enfold you, I have never wished you to meet with any evil. But for good comfort I have sent my chief-captain Michael to you, that you may know your departure from the world, and set your house in order, and all that belongs to you, and bless Isaac your beloved son. And now know that I have done this not wishing to grieve you. Wherefore then have you said to my chief-captain, I will not go with you? Wherefore have you spoken thus? Do you not know that if I give leave to death and he comes upon you, then I should see whether you would come or not?

Chapter IX

And the chief-captain receiving the exhortations of the Lord went down to Abraham, and seeing him the righteous one fell upon his face to the ground as one dead, and the chief-captain told him all that he had heard from the Most High. Then the holy and just Abraham rising with many tears fell at the feet of the Incorporeal, and besought him, saying, I beseech you, chief-captain of the hosts above, since you have wholly deigned to come yourself to me a sinner and in all things your unworthy servant, I beseech you even now, O chief-captain, to carry my word yet again to the Most High, and you shall say to him, Thus says Abraham your servant, Lord, Lord, in every work and word which I have asked of you you have heard me, and hast fulfilled all my counsel. Now, Lord, I resist not your power, for I too know that I am not immortal but mortal. Since therefore to your command all things yield, and fear and tremble at the face of your power, I also fear, but I ask one request of you, and now, Lord and Master, hear my prayer, for while still in this body I desire to see all the inhabited earth, and all the creations which you established by one word, and when I see these, then if I shall depart from life I shall be without sorrow. So the chief-captain went back again, and stood before God, and told him all, saying, Thus says your friend Abraham, I desired to behold all the earth in my lifetime before I died. And the Most-High hearing this, again commanded the chief-captain Michael, and said to him, Take a cloud of light, and the angels that have power over the chariots, and go down, take the righteous Abraham upon a chariot of the cherubim, and exalt him into the air of heaven that he may behold all the earth.

Chapter X

And the archangel Michael went down and took Abraham upon a chariot of the cherubim, and exalted him into the air of heaven, and led him upon the cloud together with sixty angels, and Abraham ascended upon the chariot over all the earth. And Abraham saw the world as it was in that day, some ploughing, others driving wains, in one place men herding flocks, and in another watching them by night, and dancing and playing and harping, in another place men striving and contending at law, elsewhere men weeping and having the dead in remembrance. He saw also the newly-wedded received with honor, and in a word he saw all things that are done in the world, both good and bad. Abraham therefore passing over them saw men bearing swords, wielding in their hands sharpened swords, and Abraham asked the chief-captain, Who are these? The chief-captain said, These are thieves, who intend to commit murder, and to steal and burn and destroy. Abraham said, Lord, Lord, hear my voice, and command that wild beasts may come out of the wood and devour them. And even as he spoke there came wild beasts out of the wood and devoured them. And he saw in another place a man with a woman committing fornication with each other, and said, Lord, Lord, command that the earth may open and swallow them, and straightway the earth was cleft and swallowed them. And he saw in another place men digging through a house, and carrying away other men's possessions, and he said, Lord, Lord, command that fire may come down from heaven and consume them. And even as he spoke, fire came down from heaven and consumed them. And straightway there came a voice from heaven to the chief-captain, saying thus, O chief-captain Michael, command the chariot to stop, and turn Abraham away that he may not see all the earth, for if he behold all that live in wickedness, he will destroy all creation. For behold, Abraham has not sinned, and has no pity on sinners, but I have made the world, and desire not to destroy any one of them, but wait for the death of the sinner, till he be converted and live. But take Abraham up to the first gate of heaven, that he may see there the judgments and recompenses, and repent of the souls of the sinners that he has destroyed.

Chapter XI

So Michael turned the chariot and brought Abraham to the east, to the first gate of heaven; and Abraham saw two ways, the one narrow and contracted, the other broad and spacious, and there he saw two gates, the one broad on the broad way, and the other narrow on the narrow way. And outside the two gates there he saw a man sitting upon a gilded throne, and the appearance of that man was terrible, as of the Lord. And they saw many souls driven by angels and led in through the broad gate, and other souls, few in number, that were taken by the angels through the narrow gate. And when the wonderful one who sat upon the golden throne saw few entering through the narrow gate, and many entering through the broad one, straightway that wonderful one tore the hairs of his head and the sides of his beard, and threw himself on the ground from his throne, weeping and lamenting. But when he saw many souls entering through the narrow gate, then he arose from the ground and sat upon his throne in great joy, rejoicing and exulting. And Abraham asked the chief-captain, My Lord chief-captain, who is this most marvelous man, adorned with such glory, and sometimes he weeps and laments, and sometimes he rejoices and exults? The incorporeal one said: This is the first-created Adam who is in such glory, and he looks upon the world because all are born from him, and when he sees many souls going through the narrow gate, then he arises and sits upon his throne rejoicing and exulting in joy, because this narrow gate is that of the just, that leads to life, and they that enter through it go into Paradise. For this, then, the first-created Adam rejoices, because he sees the souls being saved. But when he sees many souls entering through the broad gate, then he pulls out the hairs of his head, and casts himself on the ground weeping and lamenting bitterly, for the broad gate is that of sinners, which leads to destruction and eternal punishment. And for this the first-formed Adam falls from his throne weeping and lamenting for the destruction of sinners, for they are many that are lost, and they are few that are saved, for in seven thousand there is scarcely found one soul saved, being righteous and undefiled.

Chapter XII

While he was yet saying these things to me, behold two angels, fiery in aspect, and pitiless in mind, and severe in look, and they drove on thousands of souls, pitilessly lashing them with fiery thongs. The angel laid hold of one soul, and they drove all the souls in at the broad gate to destruction. So we also went along with the angels, and came within that broad gate, and between the two gates stood a throne terrible of aspect, of terrible crystal, gleaming as fire, and upon it sat a wondrous man bright as the sun, like to the Son of God. Before him stood a table like crystal, all of gold and fine linen, and upon the table there was lying a book, the thickness of it six cubits, and the breadth of it ten cubits, and on the right and left of it stood two angels holding paper and ink and pen. Before the table sat an angel of light, holding in his hand a balance, and on his left sat an angel all fiery, pitiless, and severe, holding in his hand a trumpet, having within it all-consuming fire with which to try the sinners. The wondrous man who sat upon the throne himself judged and sentenced the souls, and the two angels on the right and on the left wrote down, the one on the right the righteousness and the one on the left the wickedness. The one before the table, who held the balance, weighed the souls, and the fiery angel, who held the fire, tried the souls. And Abraham asked the chief-captain Michael, What is this that we behold? And the chief-captain said, These things that you see, holy Abraham, are the judgment and recompense. And behold the angel holding the soul in his hand, and he brought it before the judge, and the judge said to one of the angels that served him, Open me this book, and find me the sins of this soul. And opening the book he found its sins and its righteousness equally balanced, and he neither gave it to the tormentors, nor to those that were saved, but set it in the midst.

Chapter XIII

And Abraham said, My Lord chief-captain, who is this most wondrous judge? And who are the angels that write down? And who is the angel like the sun, holding the balance? And who is the fiery angel holding the fire? The chief-captain said, *"Do you see, most holy Abraham, the terrible man sitting upon the throne? This is the son of the first created Adam, who is called Abel, whom the wicked Cain killed, and he sits thus to judge all creation, and examines righteous men and sinners. For God has said, I shall not judge you, but every man born of man shall be judged. Therefore he has given to him judgment, to judge the world until his great and glorious coming, and then, O righteous Abraham, is the perfect judgment and recompense, eternal and unchangeable, which no one can alter. For every man has come from the first-created, and therefore they are first judged here by his son, and at the second coming they shall be judged by the twelve tribes of Israel, every breath and every creature. But the third time they shall be judged by the Lord God of all, and then, indeed, the end of that judgment is near, and the sentence terrible, and there is none to deliver. And now by three tribunals the judgment of the world and the recompense is made, and for this reason a matter is not finally confirmed by one or two witnesses, but by three witnesses shall everything be established. The two angels on the right hand and on the left, these are they that write down the sins and the righteousness, the one on the right hand writes down the righteousness, and the one on the left the sins. The angel like the sun, holding the balance in his hand, is the archangel, Dokiel the just weigher, and he weighs the righteousnesses and sins with the righteousness of God. The fiery and pitiless angel, holding the fire in his hand, is the archangel Puruel, who has power over fire, and tries the works of men through fire, and if the fire consume the work of any man, the angel of judgment immediately seizes him, and carries him away to the place of sinners, a most bitter place of punishment. But if the fire approves the work of anyone, and does not seize upon it, that man is justified, and the angel of righteousness takes him and carries him up to be saved in the lot of the just. And thus, most righteous Abraham, all things in all men are tried by fire and the balance."*

Chapter XIV

And Abraham said to the chief-captain, My Lord the chief-captain, the soul which the angel held in his hand, why was it adjudged to be set in the midst? The chief-captain said, Listen, righteous Abraham. Because the judge found its sins. and its righteousnesses equal, he neither committed it to judgment nor to be saved, until the judge of all shall come. Abraham said to the chief-captain, And what yet is wanting for the soul to be saved? The chief-captain said, If it obtains one righteousness above its sins, it enters into salvation. Abraham said to the chief-captain, Come hither, chief-captain Michael, let us make prayer for this soul, and see whether God will hear us. The chief-captain said, Amen, be it so; and they made prayer and entreaty for the soul, and God heard them, and when they rose up from their prayer they did not see the soul standing there. And Abraham said to the angel, Where is the soul that you held in the midst? And the angel answered, It has been saved by your righteous prayer, and behold an angel of light has taken it and carried it up into Paradise. Abraham said, I glorify the name of God, the Most-High, and his immeasurable mercy. And Abraham said to the chief-captain, I beseech you, archangel, hearken to my prayer, and let us yet call upon the Lord, and supplicate his compassion, and entreat his mercy for the souls of the sinners whom I formerly, in my anger, cursed and destroyed, whom the earth devoured, and the wild beasts tore in pieces, and the fire consumed through my words. Now I know that I have sinned before the Lord our God. Come then, O Michael, chief-captain of the hosts above, come, let us call upon God with tears that he may forgive me my sin, and grant them to me. And the chief-captain heard him, and they made entreaty before the Lord, and when they had called upon him for a long space, there came a voice from heaven saying, Abraham, Abraham, I have hearkened to your voice and your prayer, and forgive you your sin, and those whom you think that I destroyed I have called up and brought them into life by my exceeding kindness, because for a season I have requited them in judgment, and those whom I destroy living upon earth, I will not requite in death.

Chapter XV

And the voice of the Lord said also to the chief-captain Michael, Michael, my servant, turn back Abraham to his house, for behold his end has come near, and the measure of his life is fulfilled, that he may set all things in order, and then take him and bring him to me. So the chief-captain, turning the chariot and the cloud, brought Abraham to his house, and going into his chamber he sat upon his couch. And Sarah his wife came and embraced the feet of the Incorporeal, and spoke humbly, saying, I give you thanks, my Lord, that you have brought my Lord Abraham, for behold we thought he had been taken up from us. And his son Isaac also came and fell upon his neck, and in the same way all his men-slaves and women-slaves surrounded Abraham and embraced him, glorifying God. And the Incorporeal one said to them, Hearken, righteous Abraham. Behold your wife Sarah, behold also your beloved son Isaac, behold also all your men-servants and maid-servants round about you. Make disposition of all that you have, for the day has come near in which you shall depart from the body and go to the Lord once for all. Abraham said, Has the Lord said it, or do you say this of yourself? The chief-captain answered, Hearken, righteous Abraham. The Lord has commanded, and I tell it you. Abraham said, I will not go with you. The chief-captain, hearing these words, straightway went forth from the presence of Abraham, and went up into the heavens, and stood before God the Most-High, and said, Lord Almighty, behold I have hearkened to Your friend Abraham in all he has said to

You, and have fulfilled his requests. I have shown to him Your power, and all the earth and sea that is under heaven. I have shown to him judgment and recompense by means of cloud and chariots, and again he says, I will not go with you. And the Most High said to the angel, Does my friend Abraham say thus again, I will not go with you? The archangel said, Lord Almighty, he says thus, and I refrain from laying hands on him, because from the beginning he is Your friend, and has done all things pleasing in Your sight. There is no man like him on earth, not even Job the wondrous man, and therefore I refrain from laying hands on him. Command, therefore, Immortal King, what shall be done.

Chapter XVI

Then the Most-High said, Call me hither Death that is called the shameless countenance and the pitiless look. And Michael the Incorporeal went and said to Death, Come hither; the Lord of creation, the immortal king, calls you. And Death, hearing this, shivered and trembled, being possessed with great terror, and coming with great fear it stood before the invisible father, shivering, groaning and trembling, awaiting the command of the Lord. Therefore the invisible God said to Death, Come hither, you bitter and fierce name of the world, hide your fierceness, cover your corruption, and cast away your bitterness from you, and put on your beauty and all your glory, and go down to Abraham my friend, and take him and bring him to me. But now also I tell you not to terrify him, but bring him with fair speech, for he is my own friend. Having heard this, Death went out from the presence of the Most-High, and put on a robe of great brightness, and made his appearance like the sun, and became fair and beautiful above the sons of men, assuming the form of an archangel, having his cheeks flaming with fire, and he departed to Abraham. Now the righteous Abraham went out of his chamber, and sat under the trees of Mamre, holding his chin in his hand, and awaiting the coming of the archangel Michael. And behold, a smell of sweet odor came to him, and a flashing of light, and Abraham turned and saw Death coming towards him in great glory and beauty. And Abraham arose and went to meet him, thinking that it was the chief-captain of God, and Death beholding him saluted him, saying, Rejoice, precious Abraham, righteous soul, true friend of the Most-High God, and companion of the holy angels. Abraham said to Death, Hail you of appearance and form like the sun, most glorious helper, bringer of light, wondrous man, from whence does your glory come to us, and who are you, and whence do you come? Then Death said, Most righteous Abraham, behold I tell you the truth. I am the bitter lot of death. Abraham said to him, Nay, but you are the comeliness of the world, you are the glory and beauty of angels and men, you are fairer in form than every other, and do you say, I am the bitter lot of death, and not rather, I am fairer than every good thing. Death said, I tell you the truth. What the Lord has named me, that also I tell you. Abraham said, For what are you come hither? Death said, For your holy soul am I come. Then Abraham said, I know what you mean, but I will not go with you; and Death was silent and answered him not a word.

Chapter XVII

Then Abraham arose, and went into his house, and Death also accompanied him there. And Abraham went up into his chamber, and Death went up with him. And Abraham lay down upon his couch, and Death came and sat by his feet. Then Abraham said, Depart, depart from me, for I desire to rest upon my couch. Death said, I will not depart until I take your spirit from you. Abraham said to him, By the immortal God I charge you to tell me the truth. Are you death? Death said to him, I am Death. I am the destroyer of the world. Abraham said, I beseech you, since you are Death, tell me if you come thus to all in such fairness and glory and beauty? Death said, Nay, my Lord Abraham, for your righteousnesses, and the boundless sea of your hospitality, and the greatness of your love towards God has become a crown upon my head, and in beauty and great peace and gentleness I approach the righteous, but to sinners I come in great corruption and fierceness and the greatest bitterness and with fierce and pitiless look. Abraham said, I beseech you, hearken to me, and show me your fierceness and all your corruption and bitterness. And Death said, You can not behold my fierceness, most righteous Abraham. Abraham said, Yes, I shall be able to behold all your fierceness by means of the name of the living God, for the might of my God that is in heaven is with me. Then Death put off all his comeliness and beauty, and all his glory and the form like the sun with which he was clothed, and put upon himself a tyrant's robe, and made his appearance gloomy and fiercer than all kind of wild beasts, and more unclean than all uncleanness. And he showed to Abraham seven fiery heads of serpents and fourteen faces, (one) of flaming fire and of great fierceness, and a face of darkness, and a most gloomy face of a viper, and a face of a most terrible precipice, and a face fiercer than an asp, and a face of a terrible lion, and a face of a cerastes and basilisk. He showed him also a face of a fiery scimitar, and a sword-bearing face, and a face of lightning, lightening terribly, and a noise of dreadful thunder. He showed him also another face of a fierce stormy sea, and a fierce rushing river, and a terrible three-headed serpent, and a cup mingled with poisons, and in short he showed to him great fierceness and unendurable bitterness, and every mortal disease as of the odor of Death. And from the great bitterness and fierceness there died servants and maid-servants in number about seven thousand, and the righteous Abraham came into indifference of death so that his spirit failed him.

Chapter XVIII

And the all-holy Abraham, seeing these things thus, said to Death, I beseech you, all-destroying Death, hide your fierceness, and put on your beauty and the shape which you had before. And straightway Death hid his fierceness, and put on his beauty which he had before. And Abraham said to Death, Why have you done this, that you have slain all my servants and maidservants? Has God sent you hither for this end this day? Death said, Nay, my Lord Abraham, it is not as you say, but on your account was I sent hither. Abraham said to Death, How then have these died? Has the Lord not spoken it? Death said, Believe, most righteous Abraham, that this also is wonderful, that you also were not taken away with them. Nevertheless I tell you the truth, for if the right hand of God had not been with you at that time, you also would have had to depart from this life. The righteous Abraham said, Now I know that I have come into indifference of death, so that my spirit fails, but I beseech you, all-destroying Death, since my servants have died before their time, come let us pray to the Lord our God that he may hear us and raise up those who died by your fierceness before their time. And Death said, Amen, be it so. Therefore Abraham arose and fell upon the face of the ground in prayer, and Death together with him, and the Lord sent a spirit of life upon those that were dead and they were made alive again. Then the righteous Abraham gave glory to God.

Chapter XIX

And going up into his chamber he lay down, and Death came and stood before him. And Abraham said to him, Depart from me, for I desire to rest, because my spirit is in indifference. Death said, I will not depart from you until I take your soul. And Abraham with an austere countenance and angry look said to Death, Who has ordered you to say this? You say these words of yourself boastfully, and I will not go with you until the chief-captain Michael come to me, and I shall go with him. But this also I tell you, if you desire that I shall accompany you, explain to me all your changes, the seven fiery heads of serpents and what the face of the precipice is, and what the sharp sword, and what the loud-roaring river, and what the tempestuous sea that rages so fiercely. Teach me also the unendurable thunder, and the terrible lightning, and the evil-smelling cup mingled with poisons. Teach me concerning all these. And Death answered, Listen, righteous Abraham. For seven ages I destroy the world and lead all down to Hades, kings and rulers, rich and poor, slaves and free men, I convoy to the bottom of Hades, and for this I showed you the seven heads of serpents. The face of fire I showed you because many die consumed by fire, and behold death through a face of fire. The face of the precipice I showed you, because many men die descending from the tops of trees or terrible precipices and losing their life, and see death in the shape of a terrible precipice. The face of the sword I showed you because many are slain in wars by the sword, and see death as a sword. The face of the great rushing river I showed you because many are drowned and perish snatched away by the crossing of many waters and carried off by great rivers, and see death before their time. The face of the angry raging sea I showed you because many in the sea falling into great surges and becoming shipwrecked are swallowed up and behold death as the sea. The unendurable thunder and the terrible lightning I showed you because many men in the moment of anger meet with unendurable thunder and terrible lightning coming to seize upon men, and see death thus. I showed you also the poisonous wild beasts, asps and basilisks, leopards and lions and lions' cubs, bears and vipers, and in short the face of every wild beast I showed you, most righteous one, because many men are destroyed by wild beasts, and others by poisonous snakes, serpents and asps and cerastes and basilisks and vipers, breathe out their life and die. I showed you also the destroying cups mingled with poison, because many men being given poison to drink by other men straightway depart unexpectedly.

Chapter XX

Abraham said, I beseech you, is there also an unexpected death? Tell me. Death said, Verily, verily, I tell you in the truth of God that there are seventy-two deaths. One is the just death, buying its fixed time, and many men in one hour enter into death being given over to the grave. Behold, I have told you all that you have asked, now I tell you, most righteous Abraham, to dismiss all counsel, and cease from asking anything once for all, and come, go with me, as the God and judge of all has commanded me. Abraham said to Death, Depart from me yet a little, that I may rest on my couch, for I am very faint at heart, for since I have seen you with my eyes my strength has failed me, all the limbs of my flesh seem to me a weight as of lead, and my spirit is distressed exceedingly. Depart for a little; for I have said I cannot bear to see your shape. Then Isaac his son came and fell upon his breast weeping, and his wife Sarah came and embraced his feet, lamenting bitterly. There came also his men slaves and women slaves and surrounded his couch, lamenting greatly. And Abraham came into indifference of death, and Death said to Abraham, Come, take my right hand, and may cheerfulness and life and strength come to you. For Death deceived Abraham, and he took his right hand, and straightway his soul adhered to the hand of Death. And immediately the archangel Michael came with a multitude of angels and took up his precious soul in his hands in a divinely woven linen cloth, and they tended the body of the just Abraham with divine ointments and perfumes until the third day after his death, and buried him in the land of promise, the oak of Mamre, but the angels received his precious soul, and ascended into heaven, singing the hymn of *"thrice holy"* to the Lord the God of all, and they set it there to worship the God and Father. And after great praise and glory had been given to the Lord, and Abraham bowed down to worship, there came the undefiled voice of the God and Father saying thus, Take therefore my friend Abraham into Paradise, where are the tabernacles of my righteous ones, and the abodes of my saints Isaac and Jacob in his bosom, where there is no trouble, nor grief, nor sighing, but peace and rejoicing and life unending. (And let us, too, my beloved brethren, imitate the hospitality of the patriarch Abraham, and attain to his virtuous way of life, that we may be thought worthy of the life eternal, glorifying the Father, Son and Holy Ghost; to whom be glory and power forever. Amen.).

www.ingramcontent.com/pod-product-compliance
Lightning Source LLC
LaVergne TN
LVHW041501070426
835507LV00009B/730